5
Living and working from rest

Other titles in the Storrington Chapel Christioan Life Study Course:

The start of new life
Special people –special purpose
Hope – the certainty of future blessing
Faith or presumption
Hearing God Speak
Renewing the mind
Be strong in the battle
Anointing
Fruitfulness

5
Living and working from rest

Contents

Introduction

Objective

Chapter:

1   Resting with the Lord the first imperative.

2   Deliverance is out of rest

3   Know who God is.

4   Know who you are

5   Understand the favor of God

6   Take My yoke upon you

7   The word divides between soul and spirit.

8   The valley experience

9   Growth comes from the head

10   Life in the overlap

11   The power of grace in life

12   Applied rest - activities

13   Applied rest - fruitfulness

Introduction

Life and Business so often becomes 'busyness.' We are caught up with the demanding activity of the daily round. Time with the Lord is easily missed and lost.
Life can become one struggle after another.

Life and Business has become our Lord and Master.

The Lord does not intend it to be this way........ it is not the way of the Kingdom

'For thus says the Lord GOD, the Holy One of Israel: "In returning and rest you shall be saved; in quietness and confidence shall be your strength." But you would not,' Isaiah 30:15

Will we?

Objective.

"You did not choose Me, but I chose you and appointed you that you should go and bear fruit, and that your fruit should remain, that whatever you ask the Father in My name He may give you.'
                                                                John 15:16

One of the principle objectives of the life on earth, of every Christian, is here clearly stated by Jesus. 'Bear fruit.'

Our working lives take up most of our waking time – so this injunction, to bear fruit, is definitely applicable to us in our daily work, whether it be paid or unpaid or voluntary – whatever the Lord has spoken to us to do.

Success and fruitfulness are not necessarily the same thing. It is possible, indeed, required of us, to be fruitful, regardless of whether or not we are successful – that is successful as the world sees it.

The Lord defines 'success' as our being fruitful. Being fruitful and being prosperous are not necessarily the same thing. Whether or not we are financially prosperous, we are still called to be fruitful.

True prosperity was seen in Jesus –in one sense He lacked everything – yet He actually lacked nothing, and was able to meet every need presented to Him. Surly this is true prosperity.

The secret to fruitfulness is 'abiding in Jesus.' *'He who abides in Me, and I in him, bears much fruit.'* (John 15:5)   So far as our working lives are concerned that may also be described as 'working from rest.'

Chapter 1
Resting with the Lord the first imperative.

In this chapter we will demonstrate that the Lord wants us to work
from a position of rest - that means that we must first come to rest
in Him, and then go forth from rest, empowered to accomplish that
which He has prepared for us to do.

Learning from creation.
God took six days to create all the world. It did not need to take 6
days and it did not tire God out, so that He needed to rest. Yet on
the seventh day He chose to rest, to show us a principle.

Thus far we have interpreted this principle as follows:
God did all His labour in six days and on the seventh day He
rested. Therefore, man will do his work on 6 days and then he will
rest. I have no disagreement with this principle, but I want to show
you something more that few of us have appreciated.

Adam was created on day 6. He was told what his job was to be,
*'have dominion over the fish of the sea, the birds of the air, and
over every living thing that moves on the earth.' 'Then God took
man and put him in the Garden of Eden ('Eden' means 'luxury'),
to tend and keep it.'* Genesis 1:26

Adam was a gardener, or perhaps a better description would be
estate manager.
One can imagine that Adam would be thrilled with this prospect -
in charge of everything in this garden of luxury.

However, even though Adam may have been excited and keen to
get on with his task, the seventh day was a day of rest. *'God
blessed the seventh day and sanctified it, because in it He rested
from all His work which He had done.'* Genesis 3:2

God worked 6 days and then rested. Man was appointed to his task
but his first job was to enjoy the sabbath rest of God, before he got
on with his work. So it is that we are to enjoy the sabbath rest of

God. We are called to first rest with God and then go about our work.

Now we can take this analogy further. Each of the first 6 days is marked by the statement 'evening and morning were the 1st, 2nd, 3rd, 4th, 5th, 6th day.' But the seventh day is opened in Genesis 2:2 but is not closed, as were the preceding days. The Lord God is still enjoying the rest. We are still in the day of rest!

Hebrews puts it like this:

'There remains therefore a rest for the people of God. For he who has entered His rest has himself also ceased from his works as God did from His. Let us therefore be diligent to enter that rest lest anyone fall according to the same example of disobedience.'
Hebrews 4:9-11

It is Israel who are quoted as an example of disobedience. They had failed to enter the promised land because they did not mix the Lord's promise and instructions to them with faith - that is with trust. So Israel could not enter the land, then the whole generation, except Joshua and Caleb, died in the wilderness.

Our life and business experiences can follow the same type of pattern - that is why Israel is shown to us as an example. The Lord has designed good works for us to walk in **them** - not in the good ideas of our own choosing (Ephesians 2:10). The works prepared for us are our promised land, that is the place of blessing, the place of His anointing and the place of His presence. Yet we are warned in Hebrews that unless we mix this concept, of walking in the works prepared for us by God, with practical trust in Him, we too could fail to enter into all the promises of God by going about our works our way.

Footnote.
In the creation story all the creative work is done by the Lord. However, there is just one aspect where Adam has a part to play in the act of creation.

God seems to have made things in order, building up to the climax of making man in His image. Yet the final climax is to make woman. Here Adam has a part to play. He is put into a deep sleep. Even here, where Adam is involved, he is at total rest!

Chapter 2
Deliverance is out of rest

Now I would like to show you another principle. Deliverance comes out of rest.
Isaiah put it like this:
'In returning and rest you shall be saved. In quietness and confidence shall be your strength.'   Isaiah 30:15

Noah provides us with a practical example of deliverance.
The world had become such that every thought of mankind was only evil - except for Noah. The Lord judged the world and sent the flood.

There was plenty of warning for mankind:

1)   Noah was instructed to build a massive ark (boat).
Where Noah lived there was no sea so far as we know and there had never been any rain so far as we know – why would you build a boat? What is a boat anyway?
The ark was 300 cubits by 50 cubits by 30 cubits. The 'short' cubit is 17.5" or 440mm long. So this Ark was approximately 450' by 75' by 45'. (132m by 22m by 13m)
That is an extremely large boat. Indeed, the ark was 10 times bigger than Nelson's boat 'The Victory.' A larger boat than the ark would not be built until the 20th Century.

(How big was the ark? – it depends on the length of a cubit:
There are two lengths for cubit in scripture. The standard cubit was the measurement from the elbow to the tip of the extended fingers. This was later standardised at approx 18 inches. The long cubit was as the standard cubit plus the width of the hand across the knuckles – it was approx 20% longer. If the measurements of the ark are given in 'long' cubits, then add approximately 20% to the measurements given and delay the building of a bigger boat until the Titanic in the 20th Century.)

Depending on the length of a cubit, it has been calculated that the displacement of the ark was either 20,000 or 40,000 tons. No wonder it took many years to build. At this time there was no sea. The boat was a sign to any who would recognise it.

2)   ***Noah's grandfather was Methuselah***. Methuselah is famous for his very long life span - 969 years. (We have to bear in mind that the conditions in which man lived before the flood were very different, such that man's expectation of life was much longer than today.)
Hebrew names have a meaning. Methuselah means 'and when he dies it shall be sent.' Methuselah was thus a sign to the people in two ways:
a)   His name indicates a coming judgement
b)   His great age demonstrates that God prefers grace and opportunity for man to turn. Nevertheless judgement will eventually come.

It does not take very much imagination to hear Methuselah answering the obvious question. 'What will be sent when you die?' 'You had better talk to my grandson Noah – he knows.'

In the New Testament we are told that Noah was a preacher of righteousness. (2 Peter 2:5)

We know the rest of the story. The ark was completed. Noah, his sons, his sons wives and two of every type of living creature entered the ark. God, Himself shut them in. This was essential – both inside and outside of the ark were covered in pitch to make it waterproof. As Noah and his entire family were inside when the door was shut, only God could complete the waterproof seal on the outside. There are things in our lives that only God can do. The Lord also sent all the animals and birds to the ark – Noah did not have to go and round them up.

Mankind was delivered out of the judgement of evil and wickedness. Deliverance came about by Noah's obedience to the command of God.

Noah's name means 'rest'

Now this is the point - the name 'Noah' means 'rest.' God's deliverance is out of rest.

Noah's rest was not the cessation of work. To build the ark and collect food for the animlas and birds was a massive task. But Noah was not relying on his own initiative. He was obeying the very specific command of the Lord. This is rest – diligently flowing in the predetermined works of the Lord rather than following our own adgenda.

For us in life and business the principle is the same. When we enter rest we, 'as it were,' enter the ark with God, and are preserved through life's storms.
Noah was delivered because of his obedience. Our deliverance is made possible by our obedience to the calling and to the strategies of God.

Just as the calling of God to Noah was 'build an ark,' and the strategy was to build it in specific material and to a specific design, so God calls us to particular occupations and will give us particular strategies for success – they too will be exactly suited.

Not only that, when Noah was moving in obedience to his calling from God he found that the Lord was there helping him along – the animals were sent to him, the finishing touch to the ark was done for him.

Rest requires the application of trust
If we analyse this further we will see that the key to Noah's ability to enter into rest was trust. When God spoke, Noah obeyed. How was he able to obey - By faith (trust).

The ark was exactly suited to its task, for us in life and business the same applies. We will not be able to cease from our own initiatives unless we trust the Lord. It is only when we cease from our own initiatives that we enter into rest and are able to follow His direction for our lives.

Israel had the call of God to enter the promised land. Unlike Noah they were unable to mix that call with faith (trust) and were unable to enter into the rest.

> *'Therefore, since a promise remains of entering His rest, let us fear lest any of you seem to have come short of it. For indeed the gospel was preached to us as well as to them; but the word which they heard did not profit them, <u>not being mixed with faith in those who heard it.</u>*
> *For we who have believed do enter that rest, as He has said: "So I swore in My wrath, <u>they shall not enter My rest,</u>" although the works were finished from the foundation of the world.'*
> Hebrews 4:1-3

So we can see from scripture, that, a condition for entering into rest is in mixing what we hear from God with faith (trust). Then we will be able to do the works which God prepared beforehand (Eph 2:10) and which were finished from the foundation of the world.

Practical example

In order to give you a practical example here is the testimony of a UK retailer who asked the Lord about his advertising programme:

'During October I met with my two prayer partners to pray for our clothing shop. As we prayed, we sensed the Lord saying "No" as we asked about our proposed advertising for the autumn season. We have always advertised in the past, but now we felt the Lord saying He would draw people to the store by His Spirit.
We also felt quickened to ask Him for confirmation within 3 days. The next day sales were average, and the same the following day. Day 3 and in the morning the sales were low, so early afternoon I asked Him to clarify the situation in an unmistakable fashion. Within an hour of asking a man came in and bought, at full price, 10 pairs of trousers.
I can never remember such a thing – even at sales time.
Having received my confirmation we proceeded without advertising for the autumn season with the following result:
October – best full mark up sales for 5 years
November – best for 7 years

December – best in the whole of the companies history.'

Tim Simpson – Spilsbury's of Clevedon

Having spoken with Tim recently I can add that after this season they felt from the Lord that advertising was to be resumed.

To be in God's rest we need to have His strategy for the moment.

Chapter 3
Know who God is.

In order to be able to enter in to rest through actively trusting and following the Lord, we need to know His inestimable goodness.

Here are some of His promises:

I will never leave you nor forsake you.
>Hebrews 13:5

My peace I leave with you.
>John 14:27

I give you authority over all the works of the enemy.
>Luke 10:19

I am the author and finisher of your faith.
>Hebrews 12:2

Come to Me I will give you rest.
>Matthew 11:29

You have been transferred from darkness to light and from death to life.   1 Peter 2:9 and 1 John 3:14

You have been chosen to bear fruit.
>John 15:16

There is an inheritance reserved for you in heaven.
>1 Peter 1:4

I will come and take you to a place I have prepared for you.
>John 14:3

You have been blessed with every spiritual blessing.
>Ephesians 1:3

You have been raised up and seated with Christ.
>Ephesians 2:6

This is just a small sample – our list could go on and on.

The point is that God is very good, with good desires for those who are His.

Not only that:

> '*In Him also we have obtained an inheritance, being predestined according to the purpose of Him who works all things according to the counsel of His will, that we who first trusted in Christ should be to the praise of His glory. In Him you also trusted, after you heard the word of truth, the gospel of your salvation; in whom also, having believed, you were sealed with the Holy Spirit of promise**, who is the guarantee of our inheritance** until the redemption of the purchased possession, to the praise of His glory.*'   Ephesians 1:11-14

God, Himself has guaranteed our inheritance. God is good.

Chapter 4
Know who you are.

We have established the sheer goodness of God towards His own. Now we need to know that we belong to Him and that these promises of God are for us.

Sometimes it is very difficult to receive the sheer grace that is involved. Somehow we feel we must 'earn' our place. This is the nature of worldly religion, and it is clear that this was a problem for some of the early church.

Grace has been described by Charles Swindoll as, 'A sovereign act of God whereby He declares us righteous, while still in our sinful state.'

Once called and given the free gift of salvation we can rely on the author and finisher of our faith to do a good job.

'For the gifts and the calling of God are irrevocable.'
                                                    Romans 11:29

In order to enter fully into all that God plans for us we need to take on board the nature of this new relationship with Him: Look at Paul's prayer for the Ephesians:

'Therefore I also, after I heard of your faith in the Lord Jesus and your love for all the saints, do not cease to give thanks for you, making mention of you in my prayers:
that the God of our Lord Jesus Christ, the Father of glory, may give to you the spirit of wisdom and revelation in the knowledge of Him, the eyes of your understanding being enlightened; that you may know what is the hope of His calling, what are the riches of the glory of His inheritance in the saints, and what is the exceeding greatness of His power toward us who believe, according to the working of His mighty power which He worked in Christ when He raised Him from the dead and seated Him at His right hand in the heavenly places, far above all principality and power and might and dominion, and every name that is named, not only in this age

but also in that which is to come. And He put all things under His feet, and gave Him to be head over all things to the church, which is His body, the fullness of Him who fills all in all.'

Ephesians 1:15-23

'For this reason I bow my knees to the Father of our Lord Jesus Christ, from whom the whole family in heaven and earth is named, that He would grant you, according to the riches of His glory, to be strengthened with might through His Spirit in the inner man, that Christ may dwell in your hearts through faith; that you, being rooted and grounded in love, may be able to comprehend with all the saints what is the width and length and depth and height-- to know the love of Christ which passes knowledge; that you may be filled with all the fullness of God.
Now to Him who is able to do exceedingly abundantly above all that we ask or think, according to the power that works in us, to Him be glory in the church by Christ Jesus to all generations, forever and ever. Amen.'   Ephesians 3:14-21

Why not meditate upon all that Paul prays here for this part of the early church – and make it our own – as if Paul is praying especially for you and me. Then we will know who we are – we will have confidence in God.

Knowing death and knowing life

Whilst we do not hear too many teachings or sermons on the subject, it is clear from scripture that we are to reckon ourselves as dead.

"I have been crucified with Christ; it is no longer I who live, but Christ lives in me; and the life which I now live in the flesh I live by faith in the Son of God, who loved me and gave Himself for me.'

Galatians 2:20

Reckoning ourselves as dead means that we are no longer enslaved by strong desires of our own – rather we are free to do the will of the Lord in the power of the Lord.

'And you He made alive, who were dead in trespasses and sins, in which you once walked according to the course of this world, according to the prince of the power of the air, the spirit who now works in the sons of disobedience among whom also we all once conducted ourselves in the lusts of our flesh, fulfilling the desires of the flesh and of the mind, and were by nature children of wrath, just as the others.

But God, who is rich in mercy, because of His great love with which He loved us, even when we were dead in trespasses, made us alive together with Christ (by grace you have been saved), and raised us up together, and made us sit together in the heavenly places in Christ Jesus, that in the ages to come He might show the exceeding riches of His grace in His kindness toward us in Christ Jesus.

For by grace you have been saved through faith, and that not of yourselves; it is the gift of God, not of works, lest anyone should boast.

For we are His workmanship, created in Christ Jesus for good works, which God prepared beforehand that we should walk in them.'   Ephesians 2:1-10

This passage says it all:
We were by nature 'sons of wrath' due to the working of our flesh which was disobedience and therefore sin. The wages of sin is death. Result - we were living in death. Our sin was taken by Jesus – we 'as it were' died with Him on the cross as we read in Galatians 2:20. Now the new promise of God – we are made alive togther with Him by grace and for His glory – It is no longer I who live but Christ who lives in me.

When we grasp this truth we start to see that the purpose of our life is to glorify God. – You are not your own, you were bought with a price.

'Or do you not know that your body is the temple of the Holy Spirit who is in you, whom you have from God, and you are not your own?

For you were bought at a price; therefore glorify God in your body and in your spirit, which are God's. '

1 Corinthians 6:19-20

We will be able to live and work from rest when we let go of our own ideas, desires and strategies and move into the gift and the calling of God, learning how to function in the Holy Spirit.

Chapter 5
Understand the favor of God

The favor of God of always available to believers.

Perhaps you think this statement is presumptive – let's look
together at the scriptural basis.

God will bring good out of every situation

*'And we know that all things work together for good to those who
love God, to those who are the called according to His purpose. '*
Romans 8:28

Every good and perfect gift

*'Every good gift and every perfect gift is from above, and comes
down from the Father of lights, with whom there is no variation or
shadow of turning.'*   James 1:17

Just two scriptures to show us the nature of God – I would
particulalrly draw your attention to the last part of the second
quotation - with God there is no variation or shadow of turning.

Workers of the world take note!

God is for you and not against you! There are, of course, one or
two matters to get right to experience the flow of God's favor – we
will shortlist them later.

More on the favor of God –

For a long time I puzzled over the meaning of the 'olive tree' in
scripture as found in Romans 11. It was clearly the place you
expect Israel to dwell in as 'natural' branches (verse 24), yet the
concept is clearly not speaking of Israel itself – rather a position
that would be natural for Israel to be in. Paul describes that place
as 'fatness.'

So what does the olive tree represent. Revelation dawned – the natural place for Israel is to be in the favor of God, after all they were His chosen people. Taking the story further from Romans 11, they forfeited that natural position through unbelief (verse 20)

Even then the scripture tells us that 'some' of the branches were broken off – not all the branches. God could not cut off the believers amongst Israel as only for 'unbelief' were branches cut off. We know from history that the religious rulers of the day rejected Jesus as Messiah and we know that the nation was cut off and scattered as a result.

So the good news – Gentiles were grafted in. Now salvation would come through the Gentiles not through Israel. God's goodness was to be seen in Gentiles and Gentile Nations. Again history shows us that where a nation has been godly it has mightily prospered – especially so in its recognition of Israel as God's chosen people. (USA and UK being outstanding examples – though both are now living on borrowed time.)

Some people (including the author) feel that the Gentile Nations have already been cut off from God's goodnesss, just as Paul warned in verse 22. Regardless of whether or not this is the case, the point is this, 'cutting off' is for unbelief – by definition a believer is not fundamentally an unbeliever. (Though he or she may have doubts here and there.)

Conclusion - look at the picture of the Olive Tree – the sap is always available, feeding the tree with goodness. Paul describes it as the 'root and fatness of the Olive Tree.' God's favor is always available for His children.
Together with the promise to Abraham in Genesis 12:1 where those that bless Abram will themselves be blessed, we have the biblical basis to expect the favour of God.

This is part of working from rest – God's favor is available to work in you, through you, and around you.

Favor checklist – main principles:

1) **Am I following my God given calling? Ephesians 2:10**
   (This is another way of saying 'am I seeking first God's kingdom – or rulership' – Matthew 6:33)

2) **Am I content in that calling.? 1 Timothy 6:6**
   If not – why am I 'restless' or' rebellious' or what reason?
   (Bear in mind that the flesh will oppose the things of the Spirit)

3) **Is my house in order – especially my relationship with my spouse?**
   (Husbands – honour your wife – or your prayers will be hindered. Lit 'cut off.' Wives submit [literally, 'rank under' – a military term] to your husbands even if they do not obey the word. See 1 Peter chapter 3)

4) **Am I generous of heart?**
   See Luke 6:38 and 2 Corinthians 9:7.

5) **Am I seeking righteousness?**
   See Matthew 6:33

6) **Cry to God for wisdom and understanding of the truth.**
   Proverbs 2   James 1.

7) **In all things give thanks and rejoice.**
   1 Thessalonians 5:16-18.

This is Kingdom living……………

Chapter 6
Take My yoke upon you

……………..and this is the command of the King:

'Come to Me all you who labour and are heavy laden, and I will give you rest. Take My yoke upon you and learn from Me, for I am gentle and lowly in heart, and you will find rest for your souls. For My yoke is easy and My burden is light.'   Matthew 11:28-30.

Jesus, Himself gives us this invitation. This invitation is to find rest by taking His yoke upon us. To understand we will have to consider the meaning of a yoke.

A yoke is something which binds together two animals. In some counties you can still witness the ploughing of fields by two oxen yoked together. Neither animal can extract itself from the yoke.

Jesus invites us to be yoked to Him. Then, we will work together with Him, and He will take the strain. His yoke is easy and His burden is light - that is because there is nothing which presents Him with an impossible problem.

The King is inviting His subjects to work with Him in His Kingdom.

Everything in scripture points to this working together with Jesus:

1)   He is described as the head, whilst we are described as the body. Of course head and body are designed to work together. It is the head who has the ideas and gives the instructions.
2)   He is described as the bridegroom, whilst we are described as the bride. From the very beginning Eve was designed as a help meet for Adam.
3)   Paul described himself as God's fellow worker.
        1 Corinthians 3:9 and 2 Corinthians 6:1.

4)   Consider this teaching of Jesus, found in John 15: 4-5
"Abide in Me, and I in you. As the branch cannot bear fruit of itself, unless it abides in the vine, neither can you, unless you abide in Me.
"I am the vine, you are the branches. He who abides in Me, and I in him, bears much fruit; for without Me you can do nothing.'

Abiding in Jesus means dwelling in love.

'that He would grant you, according to the riches of His glory, to be strengthened with might through His Spirit in the inner man,

that Christ may dwell in your hearts through faith; that you, being rooted and grounded in love,

may be able to comprehend with all the saints what is the width and length and depth and height--

to know the love of Christ which passes knowledge; that you may be filled with all the fullness of God.' Ephesians 3:16-19

Everything points to the need for us to be living and working together with Him.

We are called to be co-workers with Him

It is time for us (including those who are called to the workplace) to know that the Lord calls us to be there working with Him. He calls most of us to stay in the same calling as we were in when we were saved, (1 Corinthians 7:20) and to function in that calling in the revelation of entering His rest. We are not called to 'go our own way,' or to do 'our own thing,' or to 'rely upon our own effort,' or to 'rely on our training or our wisdom.' Rather we are called to be yoked to Jesus and to let Him take the strain. This is rest.

Indeed we are warned to avoid the ways of the world:

'Beware lest anyone cheat you through philosophy and empty deceit, according to the tradition of men, according to the basic principles of the world, and not according to Christ.'
                                        Colossians 2:8

If we do things the way the world does them, relying on worldly wisdom we will be robbed.

'Let each one remain in the same calling in which he was called.'
1 Corinthians 7:20

'Brethren, let each one remain with God in that state in which he was called.'
1 Corinthians 7:24

Time to rethink

We have tended to believe that once we have received salvation, then the Lord expects us to get on with life and to keep high moral and ethical standards. This thinking is only partially correct. Yes, we are to keep high moral and ethical standards, but, No, the Lord does not expect us to get on with life <u>under our own steam.</u>

'For I know the thoughts that I think toward you, says the LORD, thoughts of peace and not of evil, to give you a future and a hope. Then you will call upon Me and go and pray to Me, and I will listen to you.
And you will seek Me and find Me, when you search for Me with all your heart. I will be found by you, says the LORD '
Jeremiah 29:11-14

Here is the Lord's promise to be found by us when we seek Him. There are many other references we could use. We are urged to ask for wisdom. We are urged not to make plans of our own but to seek His plans:

"Woe to the rebellious children," says the LORD, "Who take counsel, but not of Me, and who devise plans, but not of My Spirit, that they may add sin to sin;'
Isaiah 30:1

Many working people are in this position. They have diligently worked at their occupation making and following their own plans but have not thought to take, or developed the ability to take, counsel of the Lord. Unless you ask, how will you know the desires of the Lord? And if you build only in your own strength –

then the building is on sand, and it will not stand when the storms blow, and they do blow. This equally applies to church workers.

Unless we know what we are aiming at we are virtually certain to miss. To miss the target is to fall short of the highest standard. The word '*hamartia*' is the Greek word translated 'sin' in our bibles. Literally it means 'to miss the mark.'

So when we plough on without reference to and guidance from the Lord must be stated simply – it is sin. Repentance is required.

Now is an opportunity to repent and to start afresh. God will forgive, and cleanse and give a new start.

'*If we confess our sins, He is faithful and just to forgive us our sins and to cleanse us from all unrighteousness.*
If we say that we have not sinned, we make Him a liar, and His word is not in us.'   I John 1:9-10

Beware the power of religion

When we look outside of Christianity we find that many 'religions' require their followers to perform works by way of qualification. This type of religious thinking requires people to do things to justify themselves.

This is entirely opposite to the Christian gospel, which says that our qualification, and our justification, are entirely in the sacrifice of Jesus blood as a substitute for us.

But, even among Christians, it is possible for us to take on a type of religious thinking. This thinking wants to drive us into works. Even our own flesh hates the idea that we are justified by the free gift of salvation through Jesus, and wants to justify itself by works.

Here is what Paul had to say to the Galatians who were seeking justification by adherence to the law.

'O foolish Galatians! Who has bewitched you that you should not obey the truth, before whose eyes Jesus Christ was clearly portrayed among you as crucified?
This only I want to learn from you: Did you receive the Spirit by the works of the law, or by the hearing of faith?
Are you so foolish? Having begun in the Spirit, are you now being made perfect by the flesh?'   Galatians 3:1-3

Justification by keeping to rules is fleshly, and this is why so often we want a formula for success rather than a living and active relationship with the Lord – the flesh wars against the spirit.

We are freely justified already, nothing we do adds or subtracts from the work Jesus did in our salvation.

Once we realise that He has called us into a glorious love relationship – then of course we want to follow Him, and do the things He wants us to do. This is the fruit of a relationship and not an exercise in self justification.

It is not possible to be saved by works – therefore wrong thinking in this area will have us always needing to try harder and never reaching our goal. The truth is that our goal has already been reached – in Jesus. Therefore walk in that victory.

Let your works demonstrate your faith and freedom

We are not saying that works are unimportant – not at all. James puts it, 'faith without works is dead.' (Chapter 2:20)

We should look upon our works in the same light as we look upon fruit. Fruit is the natural result of the branch staying or abiding in the tree. The sap rises, the branch bears fruit. The branch is incapable of bearing fruit on its own or when disconnected from the tree. Hence Jesus said, 'abide in Me and you will bear much fruit.'

What we are saying here is that the natural result of a close and intimate walk with Jesus, in the Spirit, will bring forth fruit Thus the fruit of the Spirit should characterise whatever we do, whether it be at work or at home – these are the characteristics:

Love, joy, peace, longsuffering, gentleness, goodness, faith, meekness, self control.

Why not do a 'stock check.' How much of the fruit in you is visible to others whilst you work and whilst you are at home? How much does your boss or your workmate see? How much does your husband or wife see?

Chapter 7
The word divides between soul and spirit.

In Hebrews chapter 4 we find the key New Testament teaching about rest:

> *'Therefore, since a promise remains of entering His rest, let us fear lest any of you seem to have come short of it. For indeed the gospel was preached to us as well as to them; but the word which they heard did not profit them, not being mixed with faith in those who heard it.*
>
> *For we who have believed do enter that rest, as He has said: "So I swore in My wrath, they shall not enter My rest," although the works were finished from the foundation of the world.*
>
> *For He has spoken in a certain place of the seventh day in this way: "And God rested on the seventh day from all His works"; and again in this place: "They shall not enter My rest."*
>
> *Since therefore it remains that some must enter it, and those to whom it was first preached did not enter because of disobedience, again He designates a certain day, saying in David, "Today," after such a long time, as it has been said: "Today, if you will hear His voice, do not harden your hearts."*
>
> *For if Joshua had given them rest, then He would not afterward have spoken of another day. There remains therefore a rest for the people of God.*
>
> *For he who has entered His rest has himself also ceased from his works as God did from His. Let us therefore be diligent to enter that rest, lest anyone fall according to the same example of disobedience.*
>
> *For the word of God is living and powerful, and sharper than any two-edged sword, piercing even to the division of soul and spirit, and of joints and marrow, and is a discerner of the thoughts and intents of the heart.*
>
> *And there is no creature hidden from His sight, but all things are naked and open to the eyes of Him to whom we must give account.*
>
> *Seeing then that we have a great High Priest who has passed through the heavens, Jesus the Son of God, let us hold fast our confession. For we do not have a High Priest who cannot*

sympathize with our weaknesses, but was in all points tempted as we are, yet without sin.

> *Let us therefore come boldly to the throne of grace, that we may obtain mercy and find grace to help in time of need.'*

Hebrews 4:1-16

There definitely is a rest available. It is up to us to enter.
This passage warns us not to fall (v11), advises us that we must give an account to Jesus (v13) and instructs us that the word, which is living and powerful, will make a separation between soul and spirit (v12).

The passage also mentions the need for diligence to enter. Some translations put it 'strive to enter.' So we can see that entering rest requires some effort. That effort is directed at being in and flowing in the Spirit. Working from the flesh and from our natural abilities comes much more easily. Hence we have to strive or be diligent to be in the Spirit.

'But I discipline my body and bring it into subjection, lest, when I have preached to others, I myself should become disqualified.'

1 Corinthians 9:27

All scripture is profitable
So it will be to our advantage to dig deep and to try to understand the separation referred to in verse 12 of Hebrews 4:

Here we see the following comparison:

Soul is compared to joint, whilst spirit is compared to marrow. The scripture is using parts of the human body to convey a depth of understanding.

The soul is the mind, will and emotions of man. The spirit is the human spirit indwelt by the Holy Spirit at rebirth. (For more detailed discussion see 'The start of new life' in this series.)
The 'joint' is the name given to the place where human bones meet. For example the elbow joins together the upper and lower arm bones allowing great ability of movement.

Marrow is the name given to the substance found inside the bone. The marrow is like a factory where the three components of blood (that is, the red corpuscles, the white corpuscles and the platelets) are manufactured.

Scripture advises us that life is in the blood. (Leviticus 17:11)

So now we can start to understand the comparison that scripture is giving us. The soul is like the joint. The soul and the joint <u>seem to be life</u>, because of all the activity in which they indulge. However, <u>the real source of life</u> is the blood and the joint will not function properly without the blood performing its function.

The spirit is like the marrow. The spirit is the 'life' factory. Just as blood is made up of red corpuscles, white corpuscles and platelets, all of which are manufactured in the marrow, so all the ingredients we need for real life come from the spirit. No wonder the scripture says that the sons of God are led by the Spirit of God. (Romans 8:14)

Indeed, in the human body, the newly manufactured blood is fed into the body by little canals, called Haversian Canals. These canals take the blood from the marrow and deliver it into the blood stream at the back of the joints.

At the back of our actions we need to have the life giving blood. The spirit is likened to the marrow. It is in the spirit, that all we need for life is manufactured. Life is not made up of, or created by, our activity. Rather our activity should be as a result of the life we have found in the spirit. Another way of saying this is to say, 'the Spirit should be behind all our actions.'

This is the principle of rest. – it is in the Spirit that there is a stream of real life available for us to tap into. It is not down to our soulish activity – that is the type of activity which derives its source from our human nature.

Diagramatic representation:

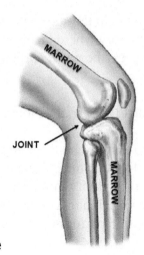

SOUL
linked with
JOINTS

Joints enable
movement.
Movement gives
appearance of life

SPIRIT
linked with
MARROW

Marrow produce
blood.
Blood gives *rea
life

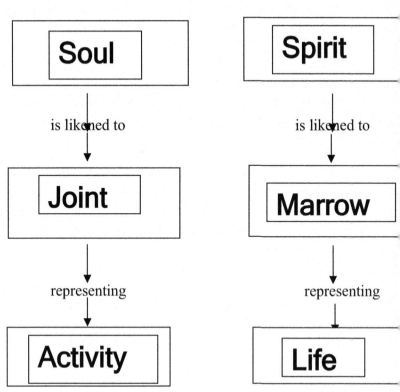

Soul	Spirit
is likened to	is likened to
Joint	Marrow
representing	representing
Activity	Life

Activity can be good or bad but life is essential.

Let me explain this by testimony:

At one stage of my life I had been following my own career desires. In so doing I had slipped out of the works that God had prepared for me to do. My career as the Managing Director of a very successful plastics engineering company came to an abrupt halt.

Now I was gradually finding my way back and I desperately needed a job. Every door I tried was blocked until I was offered a job selling life insurance.

On my first day with this company the branch manager who had employed me had disappeared - he was sacked. The Assistant General Manager of the whole Company was at the branch to manage any problems that arose. He interviewed me.

His conclusion was that I stood no chance of success selling life insurance, but because the company had already offered me the position I could continue.

Payment was by commission only, but in order to assist new recruits a minimum level of payment was made every month. This payment only continued whilst the recruit was making sales.

We were taught that our success would be directly related to our activity. Make so many 'phone calls, you will get so many interviews, and from so many interviews, you will make so many sales. For people in the world there is a lot of truth in this – but it is entirely fleshly.

However, I was rightly told by the Assistant General Manager that I stood no chance of success. I hated making telephone calls to try to obtain business and I was certainly no salesman. But for me, the Lord was in this job. I told the Assistant General Manager just that - the Lord will provide for me. He was not impressed!

I was able to make some early sales. My family needed life cover, one or two neighbours and some sales as the result of the telephone calls I hated making - it was an uphill struggle.

After some weeks I gave up making telephone calls at all. (I had 'phoned one family. The phone was answered by a very distressed young girl - her father had literally just died minutes before. That ended it for me - no more 'phone calls.)

After a further few weeks, the financing plan for my remuneration, was running dry and the Assistant General Manager made an appointment to come to the branch to see me - to end my employment. The appoinment was two weeks away.

I had completely given up on my own effort by this time. I was completely at peace - if God wanted me in this business, He would have to supply the sales, and if he did not want me in this business - then I didn't want to be in it anyway. Now I was relying on the anointing and the provision of the Lord. I only wanted that which was of Him. Now I was being led by, and trusting, the Spirit of God.

At this time I had one client for accountancy business. I had helped him start a business with advice, and looked after the book-keeping for him from the start, in my spare time. The business had grown substantially.

He asked me to write a pension scheme for him and his wife. It was very substantial and the commision was equally substantial. In fact so substantial that I was suddenly lifted into the top 25 salesmen for the whole company (over 600 salesmen at that time.) When the Assistant General Manager came he could not terminate my employment, things had changed, instead he had to award me prizes that normally took many years to attain:

A briefcase, a carriage clock, a watch, free health insurance for myself and my wife, a weekend in the best hotel in Torquay and a week in Portugal – all in one go!

Out of rest the Lord made the deliverance. I learned what is probably the most important business principle. The business reality we seek comes out of the spirit and out of rest - that is cessation of <u>self reliance,</u> which is then to be replaced with <u>trust in God.</u>

I stayed with company for 10 years. The Lord continally provided. At the same time an accountancy practice began to develop. I was being led back into the very thing I had been doing when I was saved - accountancy.

Chapter 8
The valley experience

My testimony in the last chapter describes something which is a common phenomina amongst Christian business people.

A man or woman gets saved. He or she has been livinging by their own efforts. After a while they are challenged to hand over their life to the Lord and they do so. (Maybe after some delay, as they get to understand the need for this.)

Now the Lord becomes the 'Boss ' of their life.

Its not unusual for anything built by their own efforts to decline, maybe even looking like complete failure. Previously their had been some success due to their own effort. Now, they must learn to enter God's rest and not to rely on their own effort. That which was built in the flesh is removed because it cannot stand and some things of life falter.

Again typically, at the lowest point the person gives up on their own effort and casts themself entirely on the mercy of God. Now life starts to pick up and to flourish, because now the 'life' can come from the spirit.

This can be called 'The Valley Experience' and is common experience for those who become Christians.

Fruitfulness starts here !

It is very often necessary, for us to pass through this valley experience, before we are ready to cease from relying on our own effort. Once we do cease from our own effort, then we can enter the rest of God and enjoy the flow of the power, presence and anointing of the Spirit.

This is what Jesus was talking about in Matthew

'Jesus said to them, "Have you never read in the Scriptures: 'The stone which the builders rejected has become the chief cornerstone. This was the Lord's doing, and it is marvelous in our eyes'?

"Therefore I say to you, the kingdom of God will be taken from you and given to a nation bearing the fruits of it.

"And whoever falls on this stone will be broken; but on whomever it falls, it will grind him to powder."

Matthew 21:42-44

When we cast ourselves entirely on Jesus we are broken. This is much better than having the stone fall on us, and seeing everything ground to powder, and dispersed by the wind.

The breaking of our own willfullness is an essential forerunner to entering the rest of God.

God's business plan

Read Psalm 23 as it is were God's business plan for your life. Here you will find mention of the 'valley experience' – it is not death, but only the shadow of death. At the end of the valley God prepares a table for us in the very presence of our enemies – we come into a place of amazing promise.

Going through the valley? Keep your eyes on the end – see the table being prepared for you – keep going – its all a part of Kingdom living. We are being prepared to co-inherit a Kingdom with Jesus.

Chapter 9
Growth comes from the head

In studying these things we are beginning to learn a biblical principle. The scripture states that growth comes from the head:

> '*Let no one cheat you of your reward, taking delight in false humility and worship of angels, intruding into those things which he has not seen, vainly puffed up by his fleshly mind, and not holding fast to the Head, from whom all the body, nourished and knit together by joints and ligaments, grows with the increase that is from God.*'   Colossians 2:18-19

> '*And He is before all things, and in Him all things consist. And He is the head of the body, the church, who is the beginning, the firstborn from the dead, that in all things He may have the preeminence. For it pleased the Father that in Him all the fullness should dwell,*'   Colossians 1:17-19

Jesus is the head. In Him all things have their being. The head nourishes the body. We are the body. The Lord has prepared good works for us to walk in …….. therefore the fulness of the outworking of our calling is to be found in this concept – growth comes from the head. We need to make sure that we do not lose our connection but hold fast to the head.

This is also a medically proven fact. In the human body the growth of the body is controlled by the pituitary gland, which is situated in the back of the head.

Jesus as head of the body will determine its growth. Jesus, as head of our lives, will determine the course of our lives. Jesus, as head of our working life, will determine the direction and extent of that working life. But His plans are not forced upon us. We retain free will – to choose to seek and follow Him, or, to ignore Him and go our own way.

We are called to know Him and to follow Him in all things. As we get to know Him more and more intimately, and as we get to know and understand the scripture more thoroughly, so we are taught of Him all the principles we need to be fruitful in this life. Working from rest is one of these vital principles.

Chosen to be fruitful

Jesus tells us that we are chosen to bear fruit, fruit that will last.

"You did not choose Me, but I chose you and appointed you that you should go and bear fruit, and that your fruit should remain, that whatever you ask the Father in My name He may give you.'　　　　　　　　　　　　　　　　　　John 15:16

The word 'appointed' in this verse is interesting. Elsewhere in scripture it is used in the context of laying a foundation. This word carries the idea of being laid out in a horizontal position. This is yet another picture of rest.

Only from rest will spiritual works come forth

A danger for all people, is often ourselves, and our lack of recognition that we will have to give an account to the Lord. All our effort could end up as 'filthy rags.' It is only that which is accomplished in the Spirit that will stand the judgement of believers works.

'You meet him who rejoices and does righteousness, who remembers You in Your ways. You are indeed angry, for we have sinned-- in these ways we continue; and we need to be saved.
But we are all like an unclean thing, and all our righteousnesses are like filthy rags; we all fade as a leaf, and our iniquities, like the wind, have taken us away.'　　　Isaiah 64:5-6

What could be worse than working hard all our lives, thinking we were doing the Lord's work and will, only to find that, at judgement of believers works, all our efforts turned out to be only filthy rags, consumed by the fire. The key is the concept 'our effort.' The things we do from our strength will not qualify for reward. The things we do as co-workers at the command of and in the power of the spirit will be gold and silver and precious stones.

'Now if anyone builds on this foundation with gold, silver, precious stones, wood, hay, straw, each one's work will become clear; for the Day will declare it, because it will be revealed by fire; and the fire will test each one's work, of what sort it is.
If anyone's work which he has built on it endures, he will receive a reward.
If anyone's work is burned, he will suffer loss; but he himself will be saved, yet so as through fire.'   1 Corinthians 3:12-15

Our work will be tested, and be rewarded. Will your life's work burn up or come through as gold, silver and precious stones? This is why it is so important to know one's calling, and to hear the Lord within that calling, for direction and guidance.

Without Jesus we can do - Nothing!

"I am the vine, you are the branches. He who abides in Me, and I in him, bears much fruit; for without Me you can do nothing.'
                                                                John 15:5

Jesus' statement is stunning and uncompromising. Not, 'without Me you will be able to do very little' – no!   'You can do nothing' - at all!

Now it is obvious that without Jesus we can accomplish many things – all unbelievers do so. Therefore we have to take careful note of the context – fruitbearing. Without Jesus you can nothing that will count as fruit bearing.

There is therefore the possibility that we might work hard all our lives, be successful in the eyes of the world and our fellows, and find that we have borne no fruit at all. Because that which is of the flesh counts for nothing.

'So then, those who are in the flesh cannot please God.'
                                                                Romans 8:8

How tragic, to appear before the Lord at the judgement of believers works, only to find everything burned as hay, straw, and stubble, because we failed to seek to flow in the works He had prepared for us, and did our own thing instead.

How do you stand?

Chapter 10
Life in the overlap

Now that we know we are to live and work from a position of rest, it is appropriate also to consider the existence of obstacles. Just as Israel had to enter into her promised land, and had to possess her inheritance, so we will experience a similar need to possess that which God has given us.

The kingdom that Israel was to possess was a physical kingdom. The kingdom we are to possess is a spiritual kingdom.

Jesus described Satan as 'the prince of this world.' Satan can be likened to a leaseholder. He does not actually own the earth - it belongs to the Lord God, but man's fall has allowed Satan to assume a type of rulership. (Prince of this world) This rulership is founded in sin and death and marked out by lies.

Jesus will return to rule on earth at some future time, meanwhile we are a spiritual kingdom, set in a physical earth, currently ruled by our enemy.

So we see there are two kingdoms, which are opposed to each other, both of them have influence over us and over the world. The eventual outcome is not in doubt - Jesus will rule. In the meantime there is an overlap. Both kingdoms are trying to draw our attention. Rest is only found in the kingdom of Jesus, right now it is a spiritual kingdom. Hence the rest that our souls search for is only found in the spirit and is drawn from the spirit into physical life.

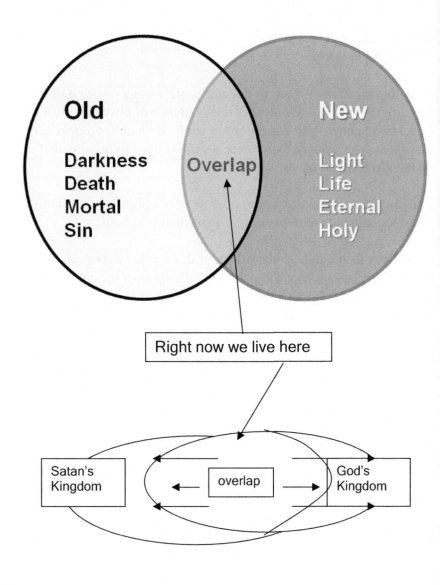

Whilst we are in the overlap, we need to learn, to understand, and to apply all the principles which allow us to enter into the fulness of possession of the Kingdom.

The other principles, which will help us to dwell continually in the fulness of this spiritual kingdom, are described in this series of studies.

Chapter 11
The power of grace in all of life

Right now the Kingdom is a Kingdom of grace – again it is Paul who descibes it – *'if you have heard of the dispensation of grace.'* Ephesians 3:1. A dispensation is a divinely ordained period (another way of saying a period of administration or a period of stewardship) and the current dispensation is characterised by grace.

Finally, in order to be able to maintain our position of rest, whilst we live in this overlap of kingdoms, we need to come to appreciate the power of this grace in all of life.
The word 'grace' means 'unmerited favour.' This unmerited favour is the gift of God to those who believe. The gift, like all true gifts, is free.

Unmerited favour means that we have not earned it and do not deserve it. None of our efforts or actions have meant that grace is ours by right. No indeed, grace is extended to us by God because we have become sons, we have become family, as it were.

Now the scripture tells us that by grace we will rule in life:

'For if by the one man's offense death reigned through the one, much more those who receive abundance of grace and of the gift of righteousness <u>will reign in life</u> through the One, Jesus Christ.'
Romans 5:17

So we can see and understand that the Lord intends for us to rule in life, and equips us to rule in life, through the receipt of righteousness and grace.

The Lord can do anything. Therefore 'grace' has unlimited power to bless us. We live and work in a society that is dominated by the evil power of mammon. We will need grace to be able to stand and to prevail.

The Lord gives us an invitation:

'Let us therefore come boldly to the throne of grace, that we may obtain mercy and find grace to help in time of need.'

Hebrews 4:16

Here we are invited to come boldly to the throne of grace that we may obtain mercy and grace to help when we need it. What an extraordinary promise - we should definitely avail ourselves of the benefits!

A study of Ephesians chapter 1 would demonstrate that the same power and might of God, which raised Jesus from the dead, has been sent to us. It remains for us to accept that, and then to learn how that power is harnessed for action. This is the grace of God, and the release comes through faith. Faith comes by hearing the *'rhema'* through the Spirit. Hence the need to be led by the Spirit – making us true sons.
(Refer to 'Faith or Presumption' in this series)

We could summarise rest like this:

- In Jesus Christ everything has been accomplished.

- The Lord has assigned to us particular good works for us to walk in them

- He has called us to co-work with Him

- He is the Head - the Head plans the strategy

- We are urged to put off the old – which represents our human nature and human effort.

- .. and to put on the new which is the life led by theSpirit.

- Function like Jesus – do the works we see and hear the Father doing

Having ceased functioning in our own endeavour, and by flowing in the Spirit, we will be in the rest, that the Lord has promised still exists, for the children of God.

A practical testimony of sheer grace.

I was instructed by a client to re-arrange his pension affairs so that he would not have to retire at normal retirement date, but could delay taking his pension benefits until it suited him to do so. The sums involved were substantial – over £1,000,000 was held in various schemes.

To achieve my clients desire meant closing down some schemes and switching into a different type of scheme. Unfortunately the three experts we asked all said it was illegal.

I was sitting at my desk just thinking to myself – 'what a pity, I can't satisfy my client's desire and I won't be able to earn the commission that would have been paid if the re-arrangement were possible.'

I wasn't even asking the Lord about it. His voice spoke – 'vote him a retrospective bonus.'

I looked at the figures. It meant going back 4 years and voting a bonus. My professional training told me this was just not possible. But the Lord was saying 'do it.'

So I did. A bonus for four year ago was voted to my client. The case was represented to the institutions involved. Those institutions who were to pay out funds objected and referred the case to the government pension supervisory office.

With only days to go to the cut off point, it seemed like the end of the matter. But the government office responded immediately (a miracle?) – saying, 'yes carry on.'

The case was completed and I was able to testify to my (unbeliever) client how the Lord had spoken on his behalf. Sheer grace. The commission was substantial.

How about your life plans and strategies
Do you consult the Lord?
Do you hear the Lord?
Have you moved into this new dimension?
Are you working from rest?

Chapter 12
Applied rest – activities

In life and work there are many challenges. The Lord calls us to stay in rest through every situation. In practice this means casting our cares and anxieties on Jesus.

'Therefore humble yourselves under the mighty hand of God, that He may exalt you in due time, casting all your care upon Him, for He cares for you.'   1 Peter 5:6-7

We need to practically cast our life and business and work cares on Jesus. This means we put the weight on Him. We look to Him for the answer and the provision.
This process requires hope – the certainty that Jesus will bless us. (See 'Hope – the certainty of future blessing' in this series.)
This process also requires trust. That is the certain knowledge that He is faithful and can be trusted.

The following testimony of a friend of mine will demonstrate what I mean:

Lynda worked for a boss who easily flew into a rage (He was not a Christian), as his secretary. Here is a testimony in her own words:
It was a Monday morning and while I was getting ready for work I was listening to a teaching tape about the sabbath rest of God. (From Hebrews 4). I was so impressed by the fact that God wants us to remain in His rest every day of the week. The speaker went on to explain that staying in rest will result in fruitfulness in our lives.
As I was walking to work I was asking the Lord to help me live in the teaching I had just heard. 'I don't just want to think that was a good message, Lord, I want to live it today.'
'Lynda' my boss screamed at me as I walked into the office.'Where are my keys?'
Panic – the boss had been unable to lock things up over the weekend.
'Stay calm and in rest' I said to myself. 'Could the keys be in the spare key tray in the bottom of the cabinet? I asked.

'Of course they are not in there. Don't you think I would have looked in there first.'

Then the boss asked me to go and look in the rubbish – he thought that was the only place left – somehow the keys could have been caught up with the rubbish.

Well there were 5 rubbish bins and I did not want to go through all of those unless it was essential. So I stopped and asked the Lord. In asking Him I promised that if He told where the keys were I would witness and give Him the glory.

After a few moments I saw in my mind exactly what had happened on Friday. My boss had the spare key draw out for another purpose and his keys had got mixed up and put away in the draw.

I went back the boss and told him that I knew where the keys were. I told him that they were in the spare key draw. He refused to believe me because he had looked there already and was very annoyed. So I asked him if I could look. There they were.

My boss could not believe his eyes. 'How did that happen.' Then I was able to explain to him that I had prayed and Jesus had shown me what had happened Friday night.

My boss - well his mouth fell open and he just sat there staring.

Lynda had managed to stay calm and in rest through what would previously have been a very trying situation. She managed to 'stand firm' in what the Lord had told her even though it seemed unlikely, as the boss had already looked in the very place where the keys were found.

There are many business situations where we can apply the same principle. The Lord knows everything and knows the answer. All we need to do is ask Him and develop a listening ear for His instructions. Then we go in and possess the land by trusting what He has told us.

Job too stressful.	Jesus has the answer.
Job too stretching.	Jesus has the answer.
Not enough time.	Jesus has the answer.

Whatever keeps us from rest – Jesus has the answer.

He has a strategy to enable each one of us to function in the way He wants and the way He has called and promised for us - 'Take My yoke upon you …. And you will find rest for your souls.' Trust Him, ask Him for His strategy, listen and do.

(Difficulty in hearing God – 'Hearing God Speak' in this series will help.)

In this booklet we have tried to lay out this amazing principle, to illustrate from scripture and from testimony that it is true.

Only you can make it work in your own experience. Will you be a doer as well as a hearer of the word? Will you be an example of Kingdom living?

Chapter 13
Applied rest- - fruitfulness

We have been chosen to be fruitful – and therefore we have an inbuilt desire to be of use to and used by the Lord, i.e. to be fruitful.

One could say it is both our objective and our destiny to be fruitful.

In order to define fruitful we would have to look at the various passages of scripture and such a study would take us beyond the scope of this booklet. So we will just cover a minimum amount of ground.

It is the Holy Spirit who lives in us and through us – so if we can determine His effect we can define fruitfulness for the most part.

'But the fruit of the Spirit is love, joy, peace, longsuffering, kindness, goodness, faithfulness, gentleness, self-control. Against such there is no law.' Galatians 5:22-23

Here we have defined many of the attitudes which should pertain in everything we do.

Fruit can have much wider application than attitude – though attitude must be a forerunner. The fruit listed above all speaks of the attitude of our heart. Any actions we take will count only if they come from a right heart attitude. This can be seen in the scripture saying 'God loves a cheerful giver' and saying that our giving should 'not be under complusion.' God is looking for the attitude of our hearts.

Here is a biblical example of fruit in a physical manifestation:

'For it pleased those from Macedonia and Achaia to make a certain contribution for the poor among the saints who are in Jerusalem.

It pleased them indeed, and they are their debtors. For if the Gentiles have been partakers of their spiritual things, their duty is also to minister to them in material things.
Therefore, when I have performed this and have sealed to them this fruit, I shall go by way of you to Spain.'   Romans 15:26-28

In this case the 'fruit' is the gift being made by believers in Macedonia and Achaia.

How do we bear fruit

In the gospel of John we will find the key passage about the bearing of fruit.

"You did not choose Me, but I chose you and appointed you that you should go and bear fruit, and that your fruit should remain, that whatever you ask the Father in My name He may give you.'
John 15:16

So we see ourselves chosen and appointed by the Lord to bear fruit. It is here in this scripture that we find the link with rest. The link is seen in two ways:

1)   In the whole passage we are likened to branches and are instructed to abide in the vine. The analogy is clear and a look at nature tells you that the branch can only bear fruit by remaining in the vine – it cannot bear fruit out of its own effort.

2)   The word 'appointed' comes from the Greek *'tithemi.'* If we were to make a literal translation we would say 'laid in a horizontal position.' Clearly the word *'tithemi'* indicates a position of rest.

Conclusion

Fruitfulness is the result of working from rest. Rest could well be described by the following scripture:

"Take My yoke upon you and learn from Me, for I am gentle and lowly in heart, and you will find rest for your souls.

"For My yoke is easy and My burden is light." Matthew 11:29-30

We have seen in this booklet – rest is definitely not the absence of effort and work. Working from rest is, ceasing from relying on our own strength, and flowing with the help of the Lord, in the power, and guidance of, the Spirit.

Printed in Great Britain
by Amazon

26632220R00030